THE ILLUSTRATED
GETTYSBURG ADDRESS

SAM FINK

Random House, New York

Library of Congress Cataloging-in-Publication Data
Lincoln, Abraham, 1809-1865
The illustrated Gettysburg address / Sam Fink
ISBN 0-679-43017-2
1. Consecration of cemeteries-Pennsylvania-Gettysburg.
2. Soldiers'National cemetery (Gettysburg,Pa.)-Anniversaries,etc.
I. Fink,Sam. II. Title.
E475.55.L7 1994 94-20308 973.7'349~dc 20

Manufactured in the United States of America
9 8 7 6 5 4 3 2
First Edition

In memory of my father, Morris,
who set me on the path, and
my beloved son, Mace, who packed
a lifetime into his twenty years.

For my family:
D. M. M. YZ. Y. L M. S. and S.T.
and Dick Bahm, who
encouraged me in this work.

Four score and seven years ago our fathers brought forth, upon this continent, a new nation conceived in Liberty, and dedicated to the proposition that all men are created equal. Now we are engaged in a great civil war, testing whether that nation, or any nation, so conceived, and so dedicated, can long endure. We are met here on a great battlefield of that war. We have come to dedicate a portion of it as a final resting place for those who here gave their lives that that nation might live. It is altogether fitting and proper that we should do this. But in a larger sense we can not dedicate—we can not consecrate—we can not hallow this ground. The brave men, living and dead, who struggled here, have consecrated it far above our poor power to add or detract. The world will little note, nor long remember, what we say here, but can never forget what they did here. It is for us the living, rather to be dedicated here to the unfinished work which they have thus far, so nobly carried on. It is rather for us to be here dedicated to the great task remaining before us—that from these honored dead we take increased devotion to that cause for which they gave the last full measure of devotion; that we here highly resolve that these dead shall not have died in vain; that this nation shall have a new birth of freedom; and that this government of the people, by the people, for the people, shall not perish from the earth.

A Lincoln

Here, illustrated and inscribed, the words spoken by President Abraham Lincoln at Gettysburg, Pennsylvania, on November 19, 1863. They ring as true today as they did then. Now they tell us where we've been, who we are and what we should strive to be.

THE ILLUSTRATED
GETTYSBURG ADDRESS

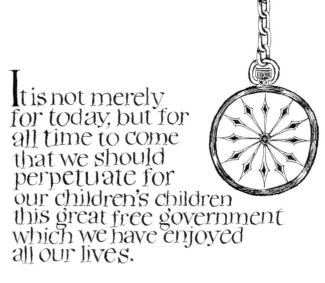

It is not merely
for today, but for
all time to come
that we should
perpetuate for
our children's children
this great free government
which we have enjoyed
all our lives.

A. LINCOLN

Four
score
and
seven
years
ago

The dogmas of the quiet past are inadequate to the stormy present. The occasion is piled high with difficulty, and we must rise with the occasion. As our case is new so we must think anew and act anew. We must disenthrall ourselves, and then we shall save our children.

A. LINCOLN

our fathers brought forth,

The "fathers" who brought us forth, the 56 signers of The Declaration of Independence:
Josiah Bartlett, William Whipple, Matthew Thornton ★ John Hancock, Sam Adams,
Robert Treat Paine, Elbridge Gerry, John Adams ★ Stephen Hopkins, William Ellery
★ Roger Sherman, Oliver Wolcott, William Williams, Samuel Huntington ★ Lewis Morris,
Philip Livingston, Francis Lewis, William Floyd ★ John Witherspoon, Richard Stockton,
Francis Hopkinson, John Hart, Abraham Clark ★ Benjamin Franklin, John Morton, James Wilson,
Robert Morris, George Taylor, George Ross, James Smith, George Clymer, Benjamin Rush
★ Caesar Rodney, George Meade, Thomas McKean ★ Charles Carroll of Carrollton, William Paca,
Samuel Chase, Thomas Stone ★ Richard Henry Lee, Thomas Jefferson, Benjamin Harrison,
George Wythe, Francis Lightfoot Lee, Carter Braxton, Thomas Nelson JR ★ Joseph Hewes,
John Penn, William Hooper ★ Arthur Middleton, Thomas Lynch JR, Edward Rutledge JR,
Thomas Heyward JR ★ Lyman Hall, Button Gwinnett, George Walton.

Towering genius
disdains
a beaten path;
it seeks
regions
hitherto
unexplored.

ANONYMOUS

upon
this
continent,

His grave a nation's
heart shall be,
His monument
a people free!

CAROLINE A. MASON

New Hampshire
Massachusetts
Rhode Island
Connecticut
New York
New Jersey
Pennsylvania
Maryland
Delaware
Virginia
North Carolina
South Carolina
Georgia

a new
nation,

...let every man remember
that to violate the law
is to trample the blood
of his father, and
to tear the charter
of his own and
his children's liberty.

LINCOLN

Conceived
in
Liberty,

Important
principles
may
and
must
be inflexible.

A. LINCOLN

and
dedicated
to the
proposition

No man
is good enough
to govern
another man
without
that other's
consent.

LINCOLN

that all men
are created equal.

If I were to read,
much less answer,
all the attacks
made on me,
this shop might
as well be closed
for other business.

LINCOLN

NOW
we are engaged
in a great civil war,

Lincoln had
faith in time,
and time
has justified
his faith.

BENJAMIN HARRISON

testing
whether
that nation,

or any nation,

While the people
retain their virtue
and vigilance,
no administration,
by any extreme
of wickedness
or folly, can very
seriously injure
the government
in the short span
of four years.

LINCOLN

So conceived,
and
so dedicated,
can long endure.

He has doctrines,
not hatreds and is
without ambition
except to do good
and serve his country.

ELIHU WASHBURNE, 1860

We are met here
on a great battlefield
of that war.

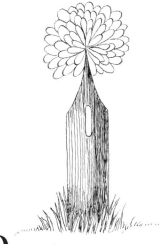

Die when I may,
I want it said of me
to those who know
me best that I have
always plucked
a thistle and planted
a flower where
I thought a flower
would grow.

A. LINCOLN

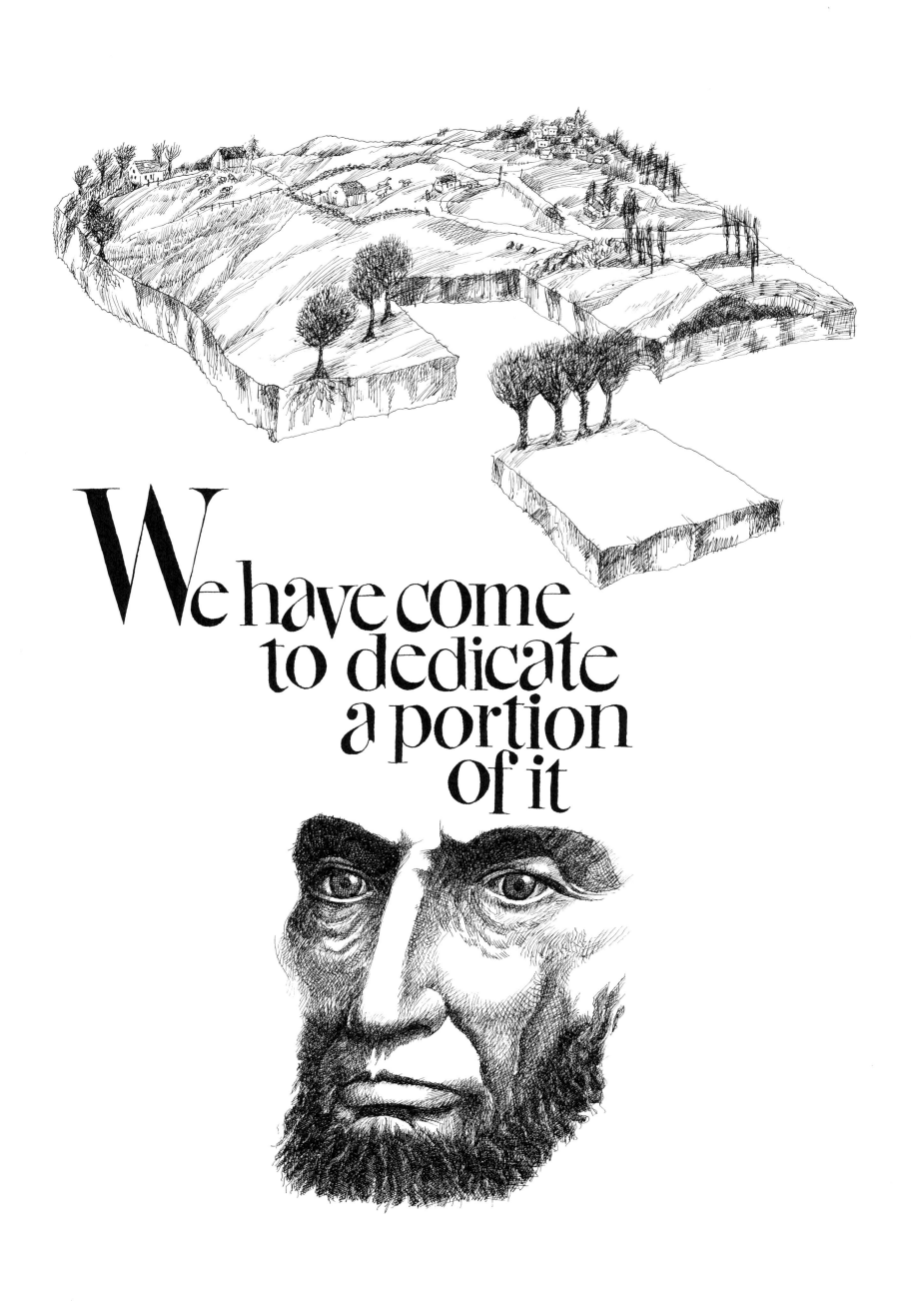

We have come
to dedicate
a portion
of it

Here was a man to hold
against the world,
A man to match
the mountains
and the sea.

EDWIN MARKHAM

as
a final
resting
place

I desire so to conduct
the affairs of this
administration
that if at the end,
when I come to
lay down the reins
of power, I have
lost every other
friend on earth,
I shall at least have
one friend left,
and that friend
shall be down
inside me.

A. LINCOLN, 1864

for
those
who here
gave their lives

His heart was as great
as the world, but there
was no room in it
to hold the memory
of a wrong.

RALPH WALDO EMERSON

that
that
nation
might
live.

If the good people,
in their wisdom,
shall see fit
to keep me
in the
background,
I have been
too familiar
with
disappointments
to be very much
chagrined.

LINCOLN

It is altogether fitting and proper that we should do this.

He read diligently,
studied in the daytime,
didn't after night much,
went to bed early,
got up early,
and then read,
eat his breakfast,
got to work in the field
with the men.
Abe read all the books
he could lay his hands on,
and when he came across
a passage that struck him,
he would write it down
on boards if he had
no paper and keep it there
till he did get paper,
then he would rewrite it,
look at it, repeat it.

SARAH BUSH JOHNSTON LINCOLN,
his stepmother

Lincoln was a very normal man with very normal gifts, but all upon a great scale, all knit together in loose and natural form, like the great frame in which he moved and dwelt.

WOODROW WILSON

GETTYSBURG

we can not
consecrate~
we can not
hallow
this ground.

O Captain! my Captain!
 our fearful trip is done.
The ship has weather'd every rack,
 the prize we sought is won,
The port is near, the bells I hear,
 the people all exulting,
While follow eyes the steady keel,
 the vessel grim and daring;
But O heart! heart! heart!
 O the bleeding drops of red
Where on the deck my Captain lies
 Fallen cold and dead.

WALT WHITMAN

The brave men,
living and dead,
who struggled here,

Some opulent force of genius,
    soul and race,
Some deep life-current
    from far centuries
Flowed in his mind
    and lighted his sad eyes,
And gave his name among
    great names a higher place.

JOEL BROWN

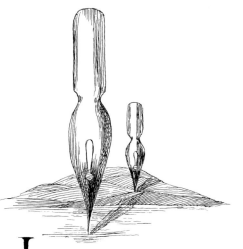

I don't know who
my grandfather was;
I am more concerned
to know what his
grandson will be.

LINCOLN

The world
will little note,
nor long remember,
what we say here,

We Americans today
are fortunate that
the statues of Lincoln
we look at have
marble eyes.
Were they human eyes,
I fear we would wilt
before their honest
return gaze.

KARL F. VOLLMER, 1993

but
can
never
forget
what
they
did
here.

A blend of mirth and sadness,
   smiles and tears;
A Quaint Knight-errant
   of the pioneers;
A homely hero,
   born of sod;
A Peasant Prince;
   a Masterpiece of God.

WALTER MALONE

It is for us, the living,
rather
to be dedicated here

If destruction be our lot
we must ourselves
be its author and finisher.
As a nation of freemen
we must live
through all time,
or die by suicide.

A. LINCOLN

NORTH SOUTH

to the
unfinished work

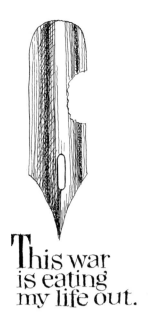

This war
is eating
my life out.

A. LINCOLN

which they
have, thus far,
so nobly carried on.

The stuff of which
he is made
must be as stern
as the aspect
of our days.

H. VILLARD

It is rather for us to be here dedicated

Addressing a Cabinet Meeting.

Gentlemen: I have, as you
are aware, thought a great
deal about the relation
of this war to slavery...
Several weeks ago,
I read an order on this subject...
which on account of objections,
made by some of you,
was not issued.
Ever since then my mind
has been occupied
with this subject...to issue
a Proclamation of Emancipation.
I said nothing to anyone
but I made a promise
to myself, and...to my Maker.
I am going to fulfill that promise.
I have got you together
to hear what I have written down.
I do not wish your advice
about the main matter;
~for that I have
determined for myself.

A. LINCOLN

to the great task remaining before us~

ONE NATION WITH LIBERTY FOR ALL

Let us have faith
that right
makes might,
and in that faith,
let us,
to the end,
dare to do
our duty
as we
understand it.

A. LINCOLN

that from
these honored dead
we take
increased devotion

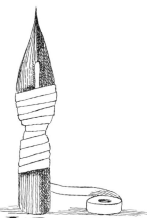

With malice toward none,
with charity for all,
with firmness in
the right as God gives us
to see the right,
let us strive on to finish
the work we are in,
to bind up
the nation's wounds,
to care for him
who shall have
borne the battle
and for his widow
and his orphan,
to do all
which may achieve
and cherish
a just
and lasting peace
among ourselves
and with
all nations.

A. LINCOLN

to that cause
for which they here gave
the last full measure
of devotion~

Abraham wore
a stovepipe hat
That brushed the stars
where he walked.

JOSEPH AUSLANDER

~that we here
highly resolve

It is said an Eastern
monarch once charged
his wise men to invent
him a sentence, to be
ever in view, and which
should be true and
appropriate in all
times and situations.
They presented him
the words:
"And this, too,
shall pass away."
How much it expresses!
How chastening in
the hour of pride!
How consoling in the
depths of affliction!

A. LINCOLN, 1859

Not often in the
story of mankind
does a man arrive
on earth who is
both velvet and steel,
who is
as hard as a rock
and soft as
a drifting fog,
who holds in his
heart and mind
the paradox of
terrible storm
and peace
unspeakable
and perfect.

CARL SANDBURG

that
this
nation
shall have
a new birth
of freedom;

SEEDS
of
FREEDOM

...A kind of passion
with me, and it has
stuck by me;
for I am never
easy now,
when I am handling
a thought
till I have
bounded it north,
and bounded it south,
and bounded it east
and bounded it west...

A. LINCOLN

and that
this government
of the people,
by the people,
for the people,

Now he belongs
to the ages.

EDWIN STANTON

Shall not perish
from the earth.